crafty
girl

cool stuff

This Book Belongs To:

Lauren

# crafty girl

# cool stuff

## things to make and do

by Jennifer Traig
and Julianne Balmain

CHRONICLE BOOKS

SAN FRANCISCO

Library of Congress Cataloging-in-Publication Data available.

ISBN 0-8118-2945-6

Printed in Singapore

Line drawings by Stephanie Sadler
Designed and illustrated by Gayle Steinbeigle

Distributed in Canada by Raincoast Books
9050 Shaughnessy Street
Vancouver, British Columbia V6P 6E5

10   9   8   7   6   5   4   3   2

Chronicle Books LLC
85 Second Street
San Francisco, California 94105

www.chroniclebooks.com

Aleene's Tacky Glue is a licensed trademark of Aleene's Licensing Company, LLC. Astroturf is a licensed trademark of Southwest Recreational Industries, Inc. Ceramcoat is a licensed trademark of Delta Technical Coatings, Inc. Cracker Jack is a licensed trademark of Recot, Inc. Ding Dong is a licensed trademark of Interstate Brands West Corporation. Fimo is a licensed trademark of Eberhard Faber G.M.B.H. Gel Crystal is a licensed trademark of Pebeo Industries (S.A.). Lucite is a registered trademark of ICI Acrylics, Inc. Styrofoam is a licensed trademark of The Dow Chemical Company. Velcro is a licensed trademark of Velcro Industries B.V. X-acto is a licensed trademark of X-acto Crescent Products, Inc.

**Notice: This book is intended as an educational and informational guide. With any craft project, check product labels to make sure that the materials you use are safe and nontoxic. Nontoxic is a description given to any substance that does not give off dangerous fumes or contain harmful ingredients (such as chemicals or poisons) in amounts that could endanger a person's health.**

# acknowledgments

## says Jennifer~

Thanks to my parents for encouraging crafty flights of fancy and to my sister Victoria for copiloting; to Tali Koushmaro, Miriam and Mitzi Schleicher, and the staff and students at Woodland Montessori Children's House for being so generous with ideas and input; to Peter McGrath, Angela Hernandez, and Daniel Archer for putting up with a messy test kitchen; to Mikyla Bruder for being a superlative editor and friend, and for giving me a job; and to Stephanie Sadler, Gayle Steinbeigle, Laura Lovett, Jodi Davis, and the rest of the Chronicle crew.

## says Julianne~

This book is dedicated to sweet Amy B., Ms. B., and all the other crafty girls in the hood. Many thanks to our team at Chronicle Books for their inspiration, creativity, hard work, and numerous invaluable contributions. Further thanks to all the crafty boys and girls out there who continue to expand our concept of what is possible, especially Heather Peterson Brown, who made her own gorgeous wedding dress and veil, and Derek Chen, who is in the garage building an armchair right now.

# table of contents

*D*oes the itch to embellish keep you up late at night? Does it feel weird to sign your name to a store-bought card? Does the sight of a plain picture frame make your fingers twitch with anticipation? Does nail polish seem like a vastly underused medium? If you answered "yes" to these questions, you are a crafty girl, and the world is a better place for it. Don't hold back; turn yourself loose and start working wonders. Crafty girls are special. You know who you are.

Yes, you can buy what you want, but what fun is that? Okay, it's fun, but the real fun is making it yourself. Anybody can buy stuff—it takes a crafty girl to fashion a one-of-a-kind, awe-inspiring, trendsetting treasure.

The projects in *Cool Stuff* will give you plenty of ideas for transforming your habitat into a wonderland, making almost anything you own unique, and inventing one-of-a-kind gifts for your friends and family. From school supplies to home décor, there's no realm of life that can't get a little more beautiful. You may want to start small with the Birthday Scroll (page 104) for that special someone or a Gypsy-Princess Cootie Catcher (page 97) to astound and amuse your friends, or you might plunge right in with the Arabian Nights Net Canopy (page 76), a decadent project that turns your sleeping quarters into an exotic lair fit for 1001 sweet dreams.

No matter which project you tackle first, use our suggestions as inspiration, not law. When in doubt, improvise. The Mexican Hat Rack (page 72) treatment, for example, works just as well on old chairs, little wooden boxes, nightstands, bookends, and just about anything else made of wood. The same tips and supplies used to make the Swamp Phone (page 44) can lend swampy flair to most any plastic object. Once you have an arsenal of tools—such as craft glue and acrylic paints—your imagination will run wild and take your nimble fingers with it.

Whatever your personal craft vision may be, you'll need supplies to make it real. Before you drop a bundle of cash, explore your options. Here are a few places to check out:

- Craft stores
- Fabric stores
- Bead stores
- Art supply stores
- Copy shops
- Office supply stores
- Big discount chains
- Drugstores
- Thrift stores
- Garage sales

  Basement, attic, closet, garage, backyard (ask before you use)

- Craft catalogs
- Web sites

Strange and wonderful places, craft stores are sure to get your imagination going. Fabric stores are also terrific hunting grounds. Good ones carry felt, fake fur, ribbon, lace, pom-pom trim, marabou feather boas, sequins, fabric paints, Velcro, and other inspiring frills. For the home-bound, a little Web time can turn up a dizzying array of Internet sources for craft supplies and ideas. As for big discount drugstores and super-stores, they can harbor everything from plain, cheap, basic frames, boxes, clocks, and lamp-shades to glitter and plastic critters. Salvation Army and other thrift stores are a must visit for weird objects, funky fabrics, and old jewelry to recycle for cool beads. Garage sales might as well be called crafty girl supply outlets. Of course you'll want to start by exploring the backwater regions of your home turf for odds and ends to reincarnate. Basements, attics, garages, and closets are havens for raw materials (make sure you check before dicing up a family heirloom).

Even old magazines, old clothes and jewelry, and what others might call "trash" can be the raw materials for unbridled genius.

Did we mention the winter scarf we fashioned out of old gym socks? Point is, some ideas just don't work out. Don't be harsh on yourself if your masterpiece turns out to be an insult to the word ugly. You are surfing the great and mysterious sea of creativity. Sometimes you are one with the wave, sometimes you wipe out. Either way, grab your hot-glue gun and get back out there. A crafty girl knows creativity is a journey of discovery.

Finally, before we get started, a word of caution. Some of our recipes call for cutting, heating, sewing, and other potentially hazardous activities. Obviously, you could injure yourself doing any of these tasks if you don't use the materials properly. Remember to let hot stuff cool before you touch it; always cut away from yourself when using a knife; and watch those fingers. Always work in a well-ventilated room when you're using paint and glue and other smelly products, read labels, and wear gloves if you choose to work with anything that isn't certified nontoxic.

You have a vision. You have ideas aplenty. You have a little bag full of flat-backed gems and more spare time than you know what to do with. It's time to set your crafty spirit free!

part 1

picture this

# fantastic
## fur frame

Fun fake-fur trim makes a fuzzy frame for your most adorable portraits. Check out a fabric store for colorful remnants of fluffy furs. Don't hold back—decadence is the word. This recipe can be adjusted for any size frame.

### You will need:

2 rectangles of fun-fur trim, each 1 by 10 inches

2 rectangles of fun-fur trim, each 1 by 12 inches

8-by-10-inch store-bought frame, with 1-inch-wide border

Scissors

Hot-glue gun or good craft glue, such as Aleene's Tacky Glue

1. You'll need to angle the ends of your four pieces of fur so that they match up at the corners of the frame (if you know that's called *mitering* you've just scored big points). Just trim the ends of each strip at a 45-degree angle (if you know you're trimming off an isosceles triangle you've just scored big points again). Don't fret if it's not perfect—the fur will forgive a few flaws. Consult the diagram below for extra guidance.

2. Glue strips to frame, following the diagram.

3. Lay frame flat until glue is thoroughly dry.

# snack-attack

## shadow box

You may have eaten the last of the Ding Dongs, but don't jettison that box! Use it to make a delicious 3-D frame with pop-culture flair. Look for a snack box about 6 by 8 by 2 inches or so, and find one with great colors and fun designs—for example, animal crackers or Cracker Jacks.

### You will need:

Empty snack box

Self-healing mat (available at art or fabric store) or newspaper

Pencil and ruler

X-acto knife (caution: X-acto blades are sharp—ask an adult to help)

5-by-7-inch pane of Lucite (pilfer your Lucite from an old frame or a cheap new one)

Duct tape (the silver stuff)

Double-stick tape or glue

Favorite photograph

String (optional)

[1] Unfold your box and gently take it apart at the seam without tearing it too much. Open box flat and lay upside down on a self-healing mat or a layer of newspaper.

[2] On the back of the front panel, use the pencil and ruler to measure and mark a 4-by-6-inch rectangle at the center of the front panel and use the ruler and X-acto knife to cut along the lines.

[3] Center your Lucite directly behind the opening and use strips of duct tape to secure it in place, making sure tape is not visible from the front.

[4] Use double-stick tape or glue to attach your photo to the back inside panel of the box so it is visible through the Lucite.

[5] Reconstruct your box, taping or gluing it back together at the seam.

[6] Planning to hang your masterpiece? Puncture a small hole in each corner at the top of the back panel. Take a length of string (a little wider than the box) and tie a double knot at one end. Thread the unknotted end through one of the holes from the inside. Thread the string through the other hole and tie another double knot on the inside to secure.

CRUNCH

Note  If supplies are scarce, use plastic wrap in place of Lucite.

# bead and bauble
## glamorama

Turn a plain-Jane store-bought frame into a jewel-encrusted showpiece perfect for your favorite picture. Start with a cheap, simple frame. Vintage frames from flea markets and garage sales work great too. Flat-back beads are available at craft and bead stores.

### You will need:

Hot-glue gun or good craft glue, such as Aleene's Tacky Glue

Store-bought or salvaged frame

Assorted flat-back pearls, rhinestones, or beads (Feeling extravagant? Opt for diamonds only.)

[1] Consider a design. Here are some to try:
- Place small flat-back pearls, one inch apart, all around the frame.
- Use flat-back rhinestones to create flower patterns in the corners—use a round rhinestone for the center and oval rhinestones for the petals.
- Make swirly or zigzag patterns with beads.
- Write your name in beads. If it's a present for a friend, spell out his or her name or a special message.
- Go over the top—use every bead in your box to cover the whole frame in a vibrant mosaic of color.

Apply glue to the frame where you want your jewels, then stick them on. If you're using a hot-glue gun, apply glue to one small area at a time, so it doesn't harden before you get to it.

[3] Lay frame flat until glue is thoroughly dry.

# pom-pom
# pictures

*From soccer to softball, whatever sport you play, colorful mini pom-poms make a great frame for your team photo. You'll find pom-poms by the bag at your local craft store or the craft section of any superstore. Look for sparkly pom-poms for extra cheer. Choose your team colors for added spirit.*

### You will need:

Mini pom-poms

Hot-glue gun or good craft glue, such as Aleene's Tacky Glue

Store-bought frame

1 Decide on a pom-pom pattern. You might try alternating two colors all the way around the frame, or using one color for the corners and another for the sides.

2 Apply glue to frame, then attach pom-poms. If you're using a hot-glue gun, apply glue to a small area at a time, so it doesn't harden before you get to it.

3 Lay frame flat until glue is thoroughly dry.

# fimo
## frame

Create a fantastically colorful frame with decorations made of oven-bake clay. You don't have to be Michelangelo to sculpt a masterpiece out of Fimo; just choose a few colors that rock your world and start shaping and baking. Consider a theme, such as island paradise for your vacation snaps, holiday cheer for the end of the year, or pumpkins and bats for Halloween.

## You will need:

Fimo oven-bake clay, in whatever colors float your boat

Sculpting tools such as toothpick, skewer, metal nail file, butter knife, cookie cutter, and anything else you can use to cut cool shapes

Needle or straight pin

Paintbrush (optional)

Glossy, clear acrylic sealer or clear nail polish (optional)

Hot-glue gun or good craft glue, such as Aleene's Tacky Glue

Store-bought frame (plain is best)

*continued on next page*

1. Knead clay. When it's soft and pliable, use your hands and tools to fashion shapes. Try to keep the backs of the shapes as flat as possible, so they will be easier to glue on later. Here are some themes to try:
   - Polka dots, squares, or hearts
   - Simple flowers and leaves
   - Palm trees and waves
   - Planets, moons, and stars
   - Fruits and vegetables
   - Letters for spelling out names
   - Ballet slippers, basketballs, or other sports gear
   - A cake, candles, and presents

2. Use the needle or pin to scratch and roughen the back of your shapes (glue adheres better to a rough surface).

3. Bake your shapes in an oven (not a microwave) according to the directions on the package. Allow to cool.

4. If you want your shapes shiny, brush the front of the shapes with a glossy acrylic sealer or clear nail polish. Do not brush the backs of the shapes. Allow to dry. Glue shapes to your frame.

5. Lay frame flat until glue is thoroughly dry.

# velvet
## *nest*

*For your dearest treasures, only the best will do. Create a regal presentation fit for a queen with gold or silver frames nested on a bed of gathered velvet. Crushed velvet works especially well and gives your frame an antique look. Red, green, and purple velvet look best with gold frames; black and blue velvet look best with pewter or silver frames.*

## You will need:

Large safety pin

14-by-16-inch piece of velvet

Hot-glue gun or good craft glue, such as Aleene's Tacky Glue

8-by-10-inch metallic shadowbox frame

Large binder clips or clothespins

3½-by-5-inch photo

3½-by-5-inch metallic frame

Duct tape (the silver stuff)

*continued on next page*

1 Pin together a couple inches of fabric at the center of the velvet to create gathers throughout the fabric (see illustration). Glue the gathered velvet to the backing of the shadowbox frame. It should be nicely bunched up. Secure with binder clips or clothespins until dry.

2 Slip your photo into the small frame and center small frame on the velvet, hiding the pinned part. Secure small frame in place with small pieces of duct tape rolled up, sticky side out. Make sure that tape is not visible.

3 Insert this whole unit into the shadowbox frame. *Voilà!*

# the illustrated
## story of you

Make yourself and your friends the stars of your own best-seller. Compile your favorite photographs and stories into a mini-album, then make color copies at a copy shop—one for each of your friends. You can write about places you've gone together, adventures, dreams for the future, or you can make up silly captions. Take a camera on a bike ride or to a big game, party, sleepover, field trip, or other outing. Then use the photographs to illustrate your account of the event. To reproduce this book for a friend, you can use a home scanner and color printer, or a color copier at your local copy center.

### You will need:

Glue stick

Photographs

Paper, assorted colors but same size, 10 or more sheets (8½ by 11 inches works well)

Computer and printer, typewriter, or pen

Colored markers, watercolor paints, crayons, etc.

Assorted decorations: ticket stubs, pressed flowers, magazine pictures, whatever

2 pieces of card stock (stiffer paper) for front and back cover (same size as colored paper)

3-hole punch

3 lengths of ribbon, each 1 foot long

*continued on next page*

[1] Glue your favorite photos to sheets of colored paper. Type or write captions or stories, cut them out, and glue them on. If your story is longer than a few sentences, give it its own page opposite the photograph (or photographs). On every page, be sure to leave a margin along the top or left side, which is wide enough to accommodate a three-hole punch binding.

[2] Decorate with colored pens, stickers, or whatever you like. Decorate on one side only, so pictures won't bleed through. You might want to cut out a paper frame and glue it over your favorite photo. If you have souvenirs such as ticket stubs, wrappers, leaves, pressed flowers, or anything else of a more-or-less flat nature, add them. Here are some fun variations on photo enhancements. Try these:

- Glue on comic-strip speech or thought bubbles.
- Cut out the people in your photos and paste them onto magazine pictures of exotic destinations such as Tahiti, the Eiffel Tower, the Grand Canyon, the top of Mount Everest, or the ocean floor.
- Add magazine pictures of your favorite stars to group photos of your friends for a brush with fame.
- Add wings and a halo to your angelic friends, and a crown and scepter to your regal ones. Or give your pal a tattoo heart inscribed with your name.

Make back-to-back color photocopies of your pages, or scan and print pages out in color. Run out a few pages as a test to be sure that the paper is thick enough for two-sided copies. If paper isn't opaque enough, one side can bleed onto the other. Photocopy, or scan and print, the back and front cover images on card stock.

4 Arrange pages in order between the covers. Then three-hole-punch the lined-up margins. Fasten with pretty ribbon and tie in a bow.

# foto~mat

Laminate your favorite pictures to create a placemat that will have friends and family eating out of your hand. And don't forget your four-pawed amigos—dogs and cats need placemats, too. To make this project, you can use a home scanner and color printer, or a color copier at your local copy center. Most copy shops offer laminating services or equipment.

### You will need:

Glue stick

Photographs

11-by-17-inch white or colored paper (one for each mat design)

Colored markers, pens, and pencils

Assorted decorating supplies: old stamps, magazine photos, maps, stickers, glitter, whatever

[ 1 ] Glue photographs to paper. Embellish with colored markers, glitter, stamps, etc. Go crazy. Consider a theme, such as jungle safari, surfer paradise, cactus landscape, Web girl, or slick city chick and make drawings to match. Or create an official-looking document with your mug shot, fingerprint (use a standard ink pad), and stats, including name, date of birth, plans for next summer, your longest underwater stay, your favorite snack, how far you can run without panting, your most courageous moment, etc.

[ 2 ] Take a trip to the copy shop and ask the copy shop guru to help you laminate your masterpiece. If your mat ain't flat, or if you want to make more than one copy of a successful design, color-copy or scan and color-print the original before laminating.

# personality

You already spend plenty of time in front of the refrigerator; why not stick around there 24-7? Attach a picture of yourself to some magnetic backing, and everyone will be attracted to you.

**You will need:**

Scissors

A photo of yourself (either full-length or just your face works best)

Ballpoint pen

Adhesive magnet sheets (available at craft and home stores)

1  Carefully cut out your silhouette.

2  With the pen, trace the shape you've just cut onto the adhesive backing of the magnet sheet, then cut out.

3  Peel adhesive backing away, then very carefully match up the cutout photo to the cutout magnet. When photo is positioned just right, press down firmly to seal. Then go stick your magnetic alter ego on the fridge—or on your best friend's locker.

# mosaic bead

*portrait*

This is a challenging project, but the result is worth it. You'll end up with your favorite photograph reproduced in beautiful sparkly beads. Use it to decorate your room or choose a worthy recipient for your magnum opus. For this project, you'll need to use your home scanner and color printer, or a color photocopier at your local copy center.

## You will need:

8-by-10-inch graph paper with dark green or black grid, 14 squares to the inch (try an art supply store)

Photograph (a big, clear close-up is best)

Frame, same size as your photo

Good craft glue, such as Aleene's Tacky Glue

Seed beads (number 11), assorted colors

Toothpicks

Sponge brush

Glossy, clear acrylic sealer

*continued on next page*

1. Take a trip to the copy shop. Ask your friendly copy-shop person to help you load your graph paper into the color copier tray and enlarge your photo to 8 by 10 inches. Then color copy your photo onto the graph paper.

2. Remove cardboard backing from the frame and glue the color copy to it.

3. Now the fun part. Match the color—as closely as possible—of each graph square to a bead, and glue the bead to that square, using a toothpick to apply. Go the distance—the picture will begin to look better and better. Don't stop until the picture is covered in beads. Lay flat and allow glue to dry.

4. Gently brush on clear acrylic sealer; be careful not to dislodge any beads.

5 Lay flat and allow to dry for at least 24 hours.

6 Frame your glittering creation. Bask in the glow of success.

**Note** Choose the color of your beads based on the colors in your photo. Because you'll want some shadows, you'll need two tones for every color in your photo. For example, to make a red shirt look real, you'll want two reds: one for the main color and a darker red for the shadows.

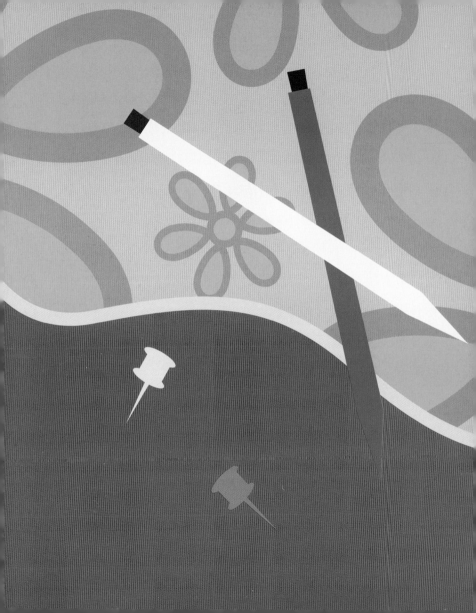

part 2

desk and
dresser doodads

# fun-fur
## pencil holder

*Pens and pencils in ghastly disarray? House them in style! Yesterday's lowly can of chicken-noodle soup is today's desktop art.*

### You will need:

Tape measure

Empty, clean soup can

Scissors

Swatch of fun fur, big enough to fit around can

Hot-glue gun or good craft glue, such as Aleene's Tacky Glue

2 rubber bands

1 Using tape measure, measure height and circumference of can. Cut a rectangle of fun fur to the same dimensions.

2 Glue fur around can. Secure with rubber bands while glue dries.

Note Use any leftover fun fur to fuzz out the spine or cover of your journal, binder, or day planner.

# mesmerizing

## memo board

Is your bulletin bored? Liven things up with fabric, ribbon, or rickrack. Any fabric will do, as long as it's snazzy. Look for novelty prints of sushi, cowboys, or Elvis. Or go for texture with velvet, shimmer, or fun fur. Then you can check "Be More Stylish" off your to-do list.

### You will need:

25-by-31-inch piece of fabric (see Note)

18-by-24-inch cork bulletin board

Staple gun (caution: point away from yourself and others) or thumbtacks

Good craft glue, such as Aleene's Tacky Glue

4 yards ribbon or rickrack

Pushpins

Assorted decorating supplies: buttons, flat-back beads, silk flowers, felt cutouts in fun shapes like hula dancers and palm trees, cowboy boots and cacti, hearts and daisies, moons and stars

*continued on next page*

1. Lay fabric face down on the floor. Center the cork board on top. Secure fabric tightly to the back with a staple gun or thumbtacks. Or, if you are using thick fabric, glue it to the front of the board.

2. Get your goods and start decorating. Glue or staple on a ribbon or rickrack border, or crisscross ribbons across the front of the board and tack in place with pushpins. (You will then be able to post your papers by tucking them inside the ribbons.) Glue on the assorted decorations.

3. Allow glue to dry before hanging or propping up over your desk.

**Note**

If you're using a really heavy fabric like fur or even felt, you're better off cutting an 18-by-24-inch piece of fabric and gluing it right to the surface of the board. The fabric will be too stiff and heavy to wrap around and secure in back.

# summer-of-love

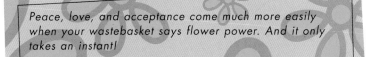

Peace, love, and acceptance come much more easily when your wastebasket says flower power. And it only takes an instant!

### You will need:

12 (or more) silk or plastic flowers (the more, the merrier)

Wire-mesh wastebasket

Satin ribbon (optional)

1 Trim flower stems to about 4 inches.

2 Push stems through holes in wastebasket. Weave each stem in and out a few times to make sure that it will stay. If you plan to decorate only the top of your basket, weave the stems through the mesh horizontally and cover them with more flowers, so the stems don't show. If you're covering the entire wastebasket, start from the top and work your way down.

3 For added color, weave horizontal lines of satin ribbon in and out of the wire mesh. Tie in bows to secure ends.

# the glamulator

Here's a quick way to make homework more attractive. Glam up an old clunky calculator with flat-back gems, stickers, trinkets, sequins, glitter, or feathers. Math is so you. Add, subtract, multiply, and divide. Groovy.

## You will need:

Good craft glue, such as Aleene's Tacky Glue

Calculator (the bigger, the better)

Flat-back pearls, rhinestones, assorted beads, and small plastic trinkets

Sequins and glitter

Assorted decorating supplies: metallic pens, puff paint (thick paint that puffs up), stickers, feathers, whatever (optional)

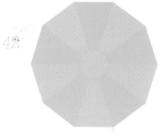

1  Get your glue and go wild (easy on the glue around buttons). Cover the calculator with pearls, rhinestones, beads, trinkets, sequins, and glitter. Leave the buttons bare or adorn with flat translucent beads so you can still see the numbers and the functions. Build layer upon layer for an ultra-glamorous effect.

If you like, embellish further with metallic pens, puff paint, stickers, or feathers.

3 Let everything dry overnight before using. Then calculate the thrills ahead.

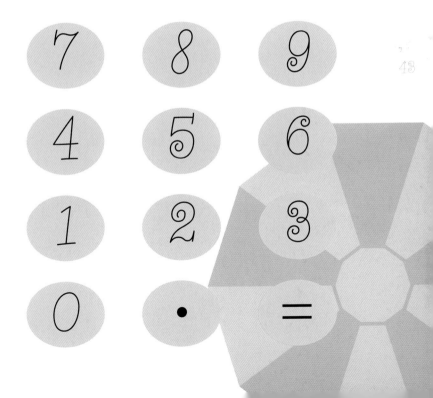

# phone

*Go buggy for a phone covered in goopy "slime" paint and plastic critters. A phone encrusted with insects insures that no one answers but you.*

## You will need:

Phone (an older model is best)

Sponge brush

Bright-green translucent acrylic paint (Pebeo Gel Crystal is a good brand)

Good craft glue, such as Aleene's Tacky Glue

Plastic bugs

Bright-green phone cord (optional)

1 Unplug the phone. Make sure it is clean and dry. Using the sponge brush, paint handset and receiver with green paint. Don't worry about a smooth finish—the goopier and gunkier, the better. Avoid the holes and buttons and other important stuff.

44

2  Allow to dry. (If it rings, don't answer.)

3  Glue on plastic bugs as desired.

4  Replace the cord with a bright-green one (available at hardware stores) for a truly organic effect.

*Note*

Fear of insects getting you down? Swap the green paint with blue, and forego the bugs in favor of colorful plastic fish. Mermaids need phones, too.

# movie-star phone

*Ring, ring, ring; everyone wants to talk to you, and no ordinary phone will do. You need a jeweled one, dahling. Make it yourself with flat-back rhinestones, glitter, and paint.*

### You will need:

Phone (unplugged)

Good craft glue, such as Aleene's Tacky Glue

Flat-back rhinestones, pearls, or beads

Shimmery gold paint (use a nontoxic metallic acrylic, like Ceramcoat Gleams)

1. Make sure phone is clean and dry. Glue on rhinestones, pearls, or beads. Here are some designs to try:
   - Cover every bit of the phone for a jewel-encrusted showpiece.
   - Make a delicate flower pattern, using the beads and pearls.
   - Circle the number pad with a big, shiny rhinestone heart.
   - Write your name or initials in tiny rhinestones or beads.
   - Paint the phone gold, allow to dry, then judiciously apply a few dazzling rhinestones or pearls.

2. Allow to dry completely before using. As this could take well over an hour, arrange to have another phone on hand in case of an emergency, such as a call from your agent.

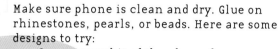

# pearly

## jewel box

48

> *House your booty in an opulent treasure chest. Simply paint a plain wood or papier-mâché box (available in craft stores) and add pearl feet and a pearl pull.*

**You will need:**

Sponge brush

Unfinished wood or papier-mâché box

Pearlized acrylic craft paint (pearl white, gray, blue, and pink are all especially pretty)

Good craft glue, such as Aleene's Tacky Glue

5 pearls, size 12 mm or larger

1   Using the sponge brush, paint box with pearly paint. You'll probably need several coats. Be sure to let it dry well between coats, and be careful not to paint the box shut.

2   When you're satisfied with the color and the paint is thoroughly dry, glue four pearl feet to the bottom of the box (one in each corner if the box is square, or equidistant around the perimeter if it's round).

3   Glue a pearl to the center of the top, let dry, and find a place of honor for your new creation.

# box yourself in

Put your mementos outside a box as well as in it. Thanks to the miracle of découpage, your pictures, postcards, and drawings, as well as secret notes, lace, and other souvenirs, can become one with any box to make a unique hideaway for all your keepsakes.

### You will need:

Box (wood, papier-mâché, whatever—even a shoe box will work)

Glue stick

Assorted decorating supplies: pictures, notes, ticket stubs, stickers, stamps, wrappers, drawings, newspaper or magazine headlines, or anything you want to seal in forever

Sponge brush

Découpage medium (for example, Modge Podge)

Glossy, clear acrylic sealer (optional)

1 Make sure box is clean and dry. Using glue stick, arrange and adhere your decorations to the surfaces of the box, as desired.

continued on next page

2   Using sponge brush, seal the outside of the box with a coat of découpage medium, carefully painting over the decorations. Be careful not to seal the box shut. Allow to dry.

3   Apply more coats of découpage medium as necessary. Use enough to make the pictures and other items adhere well, but not so much that it makes them bumpy. Allow to dry well between coats.

4   If desired, you can finish with a coat of clear acrylic sealer for extra gloss.

*Note*   The same treatment will work for the cover of your binder or for just about any other hard surface.

# custom
# calendar

Make every day your day! Use your favorite photographs to create a calendar for the whole year. Design it to match your room, to celebrate your favorite animal, sport, or hobby, or as a surprise for your best friends and family. Custom Calendars make great gifts around the holidays because it is easy to run off as many copies as you like. For this project, you'll need to use your home scanner and color printer, or a color photocopier at your local copy center.

## You will need:

25 sheets 8½-by-11-inch paper
(colored or white) for originals

Pen and ruler

Glue stick

13 photographs

Assorted decorating supplies: colored
pens, glitter, stickers, stamps, whatever

13 sheets sturdy white copy paper for
each additional calendar

3-hole paper punch

3 pieces of narrow ribbon

Regular paper punch

continued on next page

[1] Make a grid for each month on a separate sheet of paper. If you would rather do this step on your computer, you can use your word-processing program to create calendar pages. Otherwise, draw them by hand with a pen and ruler, using another calendar as your guide. Leave at least a 1-inch border at the top and bottom of your grid (for the hole punching that happens later). You may want to mark any important dates, such as birthdays and holidays.

[2] Create a picture page for each month. Use a glue stick to tack down your photographs as desired, then decorate page with colored pens, stickers, glitter, or whatever you like. Leave a border at the top and bottom of the sheet (again, for the hole punching).

[3] Make a colorful cover page for your calendar, just like in step 2.

4 Color-copy, or scan and print out, your originals
on the heavy stock, double-sided, as follows:

- Cover/January picture
- January grid/February picture
- February grid/March picture
- March grid/April picture
- April grid/May picture
- May grid/June picture
- June grid/July picture
- July grid/August picture
- August grid/September picture
- September grid/October picture
- October grid/November picture
- November grid/December picture
- December grid/Back cover

Be sure that the front of each page (the grid) is
right side up and the back of the page (the art) is
upside down. Study a store-bought calendar for
further clarification. Also, make sure the paper
that you're copying onto is thick enough so images
and type won't bleed through to the other side.

5 Arrange your pages in order and three-hole-
punch the top edge. Thread ribbon through
each set of holes and tie together in a bow.

6 For hanging your calendar, use the single-
hole punch to make one hole on the bottom of
each page and cover of the calendar; make
sure the holes line up. It's a brand new year!

# time to
## shine

Sound the alarm, it's high time to make a statement with your own spectacularly personalized clock. Every clock has a face; now it can have yours! Take a no-frills plastic wall clock from a superstore or drugstore and transform it into a timeless timepiece in just minutes.

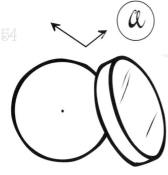

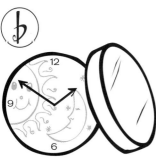

### You will need:

10-inch cheap-o round wall clock

Butter knife

Heavy paper or poster board, at least 10 by 10 inches (for clock face)

Pencil

Scissors

Self-healing mat (available at art or fabric store), or newspapers

X-acto knife (caution: X-acto blades are sharp—ask an adult to help)

Glue

Photos, stickers, paints, and other art supplies to decorate with

1. Carefully remove the clear plastic cover of the clock. If it doesn't pop out easily, you should be able to jimmy it off by wedging a butter knife between the cover and the rim of the clock. It's fairly easy to crack the plastic cover and rim, so proceed gently. Set cover aside. Carefully remove the clock hands and paper clock-face and set aside (see diagram a).

2. Using the paper clock-face you just removed as a pattern, trace its shape on the heavy paper or poster board, and mark the center. This will be your new clock-face; now you can cut it out. Using the old paper clock-face again as a guide, lightly mark the placement of the numbers on the new face. On a self-healing mat or a short stack of newspapers, use the X-acto knife to cut a small hole out of the center (this is for the mechanism that holds the hands).

3. Decorate the new face, gluing on photos and adding stickers, as desired. Maybe a small picture of you can replace the number 12, and your three best pals are at 3:00, 6:00, and 9:00. Or how about a photo of a large smiling face—maybe yours truly. Whatever makes you tick. Add fancy hand-drawn numbers for extra panache.

4. Place the newly decorated face on the clock base, making sure 12 o'clock is at the top, and the mechanism is lined up with the hole (see diagram b). Replace clock hands and plastic cover and install where every minute counts.

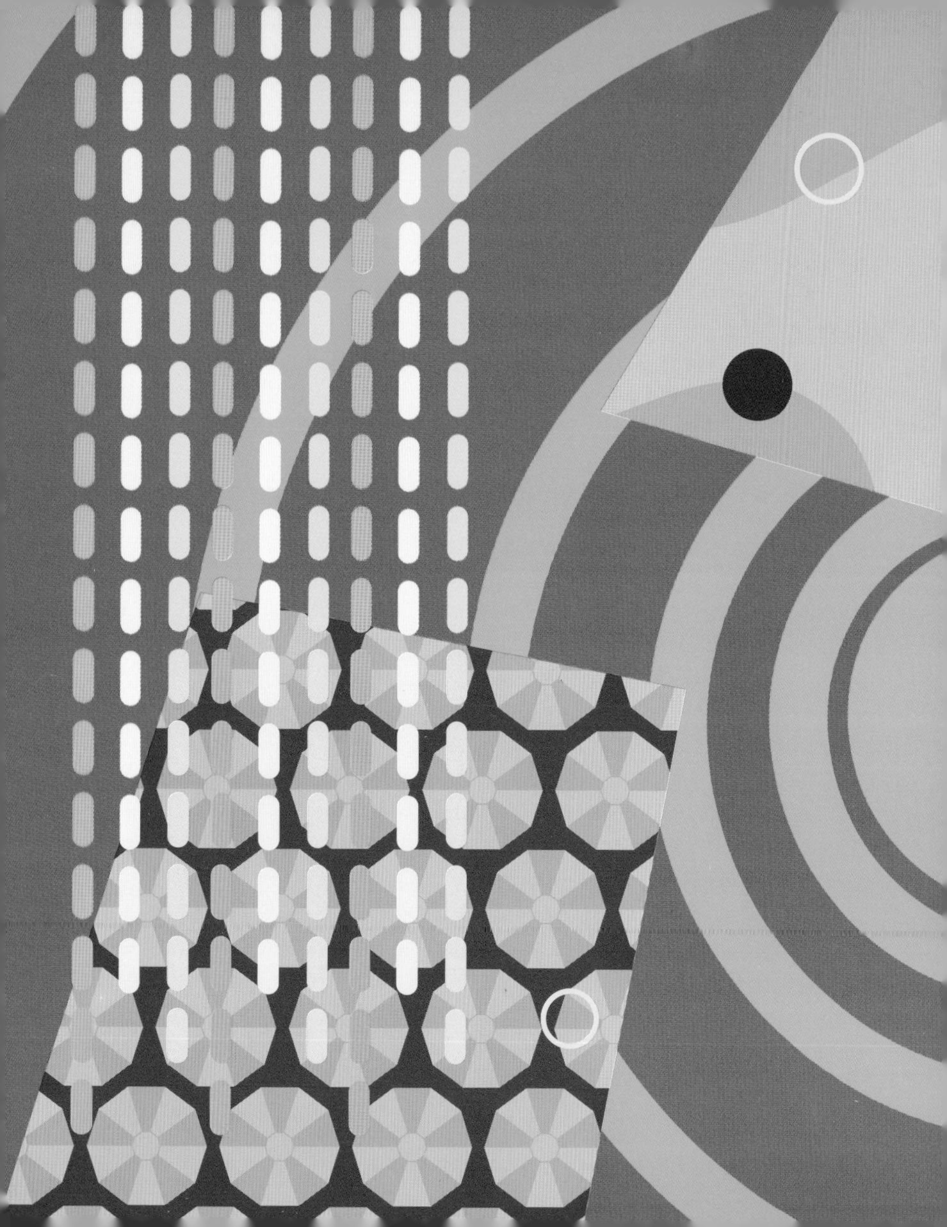

part 3

wonderful windows,
walls, and doors

# doors of perception

Part barrier, part grand entrance, the door to your room should hint at the wonders—or perils—that lie behind it. A dirty T-shirt hanging from the knob may be its only decoration right now, but soon it can look like a portal to magic and mystery. Here are five ideas. Do with them what you will.

## You will need any or all of the following:

Pictures or photos

Glue stick

Découpage medium and sponge brush, or clear nail polish

Craft paint

Butcher paper

Scissors

Markers

Glitter and sequins

Masking tape or pushpins

Heavy-duty aluminum foil

Glow stars (available at craft stores)

Felt

Fabric paint

Velcro dots

Ribbon or rickrack

Adhesive-backed hooks

Wall-mount adhesive gum, such as
Fun-Tak (also from the craft store)

Plastic flowers or creatures

## ❋ Découpage Door

**Do not Enter!**

You're crafty, not crazy, so you probably
won't be able to do this one until you're pay-
ing your own rent, and even then only if
you're willing to forfeit your security deposit.
But maybe your parents really, really believe
in personal expression. If they say go for it,
here's what you do: Mount your favorite photos on your door with a glue stick, then brush
découpage medium on top to seal. Use gold
craft paint to paint frames around the pictures. Then add some more craft paint and
embellish further. Paint palm trees, lines of
poetry, pyramids, eyeballs, or the Eiffel
Tower—whatever butters your baguette.

*continued on next page*

## The Sane Alternative

If your folks nix the découpage door (and won't accept a downgrade to a sweet stencil treatment, either), here's what you do. Cut a piece of butcher paper—or brown wrapping paper—the size of your door. Then get markers, paint, glitter, sequins, photos, and magazine clippings and start decorating the paper. Draw a life-size self-portrait. Or découpage photos, then draw frames around them. Glue on glitter or sequins. When your designs are done and dry, secure butcher paper to door with masking tape or pushpins (whichever won't get you into hot water).

## Space Gate

This one's definitely out there. Tape sheets of heavy-duty aluminum foil to the length of your door. Glue on space-age decorations: images of solar systems, planets, space ships, glow-in-the-dark stars, and aliens (of course).

## The Royal Treatment

Felt is inexpensive and comes in a rainbow of colors. Requisition a large piece and some sticky-backed Velcro dots from a craft or fabric store. Use a marker or fabric paint to inscribe *The Queen of this kingdom is . . .* in your most regal handwriting. On smaller pieces of felt, inscribe *Having a Royal Nap*; *Receiving Humble Visitors*; *Out Surveying Her Kingdom and Attending to Affairs of State*; *Retired for the Eve*; *Sulking*; or whatever her majesty pleases. Attach two Velcro dots to the back of each small felt piece, and attach one set of corresponding Velcro dots to the large piece of felt. Now you can keep the kingdom informed any time of day or night. Decorate your felt tapestry even more by gluing on ribbon or rickrack, if you like. Hang your tapestry on your door with pushpins. Or, to avoid the dreaded holes in the woodwork, sew two ribbon loops on the back of your tapestry, stick adhesive-backed hooks on your door, and hang tapestry from loops.

## Creature Garden

Seek blessing from the powers that be before commencing work on this masterpiece. Then paint your door a springy green or sky blue, or blue on top and green on the bottom. Use wads of Fun-Tak to affix plastic flowers or creatures to your door. Make a nature-inspired tableau with plastic frogs chasing plastic flies, plastic ants hunting plastic sushi, and plastic butterflies floating over plastic flowers. If there still isn't enough going on, paint some trees, a sun, puffy clouds, a pond, more flowers, and maybe a butterfly or two.

# illustrated
## curtain

There's no reason you can't have a spectacular view even when your curtain is drawn. Replace your humdrum curtains with a collaged curtain that gives you loads to look at. Peruse old magazines for a fashion, fitness, or travel motif. If you're a skateboard or surfing fanatic, use magazine pictures of your dream rides and maneuvers. Or grab a horse, cat, or dog magazine for a window full of furry friends. If you're inspired, use your own drawings and paintings.

### You will need:

Glue

Approximately 54 magazine pages (so start tearing out the cool ones now)

Construction paper in various colors

Transparent shower curtain

Scissors

Clear tape

1 Glue magazine photos or original art to construction paper.

2 Lay the shower curtain face down on the floor. If necessary, trim curtain to fit the dimensions of your window.

3 Tape art panels securely face down, until the whole curtain is covered.

4 Decide whether you want the cool side to face in or out, then hang your crazy curtain on your existing curtain rod.

# the beads go on

*Fringe, baby. Trim. Visual enhancement. You get the picture. And you don't need to stress about a lot of details. Just sit back, thread some beads, and tack them to whatever element of your room is getting you down—doorway, window, bed, or whatever. But be sure to check with the parental establishment before you put a lot of holes in the woodwork. Could be a bummer.*

### You will need:

Needle and thread

A bunch of beads (big plastic ones with small holes work best; handy crafters can also use buttons)

Scissors

Box of pushpins

[1] Using the needle and thread (make sure it is knotted securely before you start), string about 3 inches of beads. Tie off and clip ends.

$2$ Put a pushpin through the knot and secure to doorway, windowframe, or furniture.

$3$ Repeat until your fringe looks righteous.

*Note*

Instead of tying off and clipping each strand of beads, stitch the beginning and end of the finished strand to a length of velvet ribbon. Tape (or pin, if you can negotiate with the management for the rights to some holes) the bedecked ribbons in place.

# poster

Polish

> *You love your collection of posters. You love the superstars on them. But next to all your other crafty projects, they look a little, well, dull. Here's a treatment to restore their luster.*

### You will need:

Yardstick or tape measure

Poster

Foam core (available at craft stores)

X-acto knife (caution: X-acto blades are sharp—ask an adult to help you)

Ruler

Glue stick

Assorted decorating supplies: construction paper, heavy-duty aluminum foil, paper flowers, flat-back rhinestones, whatever

1   Measure your poster. Using the X-acto knife and ruler, cut a piece of foam core the same size. This can be a bit laborious. Get an adult to help or, better yet, take your poster dimensions to the craft store and ask them to cut a piece of foam core to size.

2   Apply glue stick liberally to foam core and position poster on top, matching edges. Press firmly to seal. Smooth out any wrinkles or bubbles.

3   Now your poster is 3-D and ever so polished. But a crafty girl hears when something cries out for more embellishment. Glue on a frame made from beautiful paper or heavy-duty aluminum foil. Glue paper flowers or flat-back rhinestones around the border. Your stars are really sparkling now.

# make a
## switch

*Walls are for art and not for anything plain, beige, or plastic. Enlighten your old, plastic light-switch plate with a collage of decadent bohemian artifacts. A handful of flat-back gems, some winsome clippings from the latest edition of your favorite magazine, and a bit of gold paint will make your switch pasha-perfect.*

### You will need:

Light-switch plate (see step 1)

Assorted decorating supplies: acrylic paints, nontoxic metallic paints (such as Ceramcoat Gleams), flat-back gems, photographs, magazine clippings, and scraps of velvet ribbon

Hot-glue gun or good craft glue, such as Aleene's Tacky Glue

Découpage medium

1  After an adult removes the switch plate from the wall, make sure it is clean and dry.

2. Decorate in any way you like, using whatever materials you can find. Go literary and add a snip of paper with a quote from an illuminating book or good ol' Will Shakespeare ("What light through yonder window breaks?"). For an ultra-luxe bohemian effect, glue on a smattering of pictures cut from magazines, then brush with several coats of découpage medium. When completely dry, glue on a border of flat-back gems. Add beads, ribbon, or swirls of metallic paint.

3. Allow to dry. Get an adult to reaffix the switch plate to the wall.

4. On. Off. On. Off. On. Off.

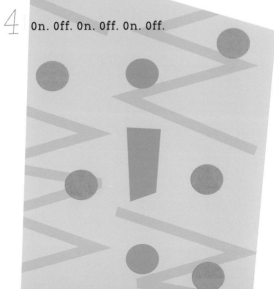

# renaissance

Days past, it was your favorite ride. Now it's furniture. When it's time to retire your old skateboard, don't trash it; transform it into an extreme footstool or wall-mounted shelf. The mood is strictly street for the girl who has a way with wheels.

## You will need:

Retired skateboard

Paintbrush

Acrylic craft paint and/or stickers

Two 8-inch lengths of 2-by-4-inch pine

Clear acrylic sealer and sponge brush (optional)

Hammer and nails

1   Remove everything from the skateboard: trucks, wheels, grip tape, handrails, and whatever else you've got on there (unless you want it to be part of your oeuvre forever). A little splash of fingernail polish remover should help get off the sticker residue. When the skateboard is clean and dry, decorate it with paint or stickers.

2   Paint the lengths of pine and allow to dry.

3   Use sponge brush to apply clear acrylic sealer
    to skateboard and wood if you want them
    shiny. Allow to dry.

4   Center wood under holes left by the trucks.
    Hammer nails through holes from the top to
    secure wood to skateboard.

5   Now, relax and put your feet up on that awe-
    some footstool.

Note    If you decide to make a shelf, nab an adult who is
        handy with a drill to wall-mount your skateboard. Have
        the drill-wielder install wall-mount shelf brackets
        (cheap, available at any hardware store). Put your
        skateboard on top. You may need to drill holes in the
        board to attach it to the brackets.

# hat rack

A demure thrift-store hat or coat rack—or a simple, inexpensive new one—shows its sassy side when you give it the south-of-the-border treatment with a burst of colorful paint and pom-pom trim. Paint it loud and proud.

## You will need:

Unfinished wall-mounted wooden coat or hat rack (sold at craft stores and superstores)

White base paint (optional)

Paintbrushes of various sizes

Acrylic paint in assorted bright colors

Mexican folk-art book (optional; check the library)

Good craft glue, such as Aleene's Tacky Glue

Pom-pom trim

1  Make sure rack is clean and dry. If it's dark wood, consider giving it a base coat of white paint.

72

[2] Using the paintbrushes, acrylic paint, and your wild creative impulses, jazz up your coat rack. Here are some ideas:

- Paint squiggles, zigzags, stripes, dots, snakes, suns, cacti, or sunflowers.
- Flip through your folk-art book for pattern ideas, or copy patterns from any Mexican or Santa Fe–style blankets, pottery, or folk art you may have around the house.
- Paint Day-of-the-Dead skeleton figures.
- Alternate red and yellow stripes. Purple and green, hot pink and green, and yellow and purple also look good.

[3] Allow paint to dry.

[4] Glue pom-pom trim across the top or bottom, let dry, and hang your hat, señorita.

part 4
sleep tight

# net canopy

A fluffy confection of gauzy net surrounds your bed to keep out insects, siblings, and other pests. One thousand and one splendid nights await you inside your dreamy retreat, and each morning you will wake to pale light filtered through a screen of white. Caution: First, you'll need a tall adult (or one with a ladder) to help you install the ceiling hook. Second, this project requires an armload of netting. The fabric-store employees may think you're crazy, but consider how cool your canopy will look and remember that netting is only going to set you back about fifty cents a yard. Crazy like a fox.

## You will need:

Large ceiling-mount hook

3 lengths of ribbon, each 2 yards long (longer if you have a high ceiling)

Lightweight 12-inch hoop (plastic, wood, or metal)

Ball of string or measuring tape

Scissors

36 yards (approximately) cheap, white netting

Silk or plastic flowers (optional)

Silk or plastic butterflies (optional)

Needle and thread

[1] Have an adult install the hook in your ceiling, smack-dab over the middle of your bed. Loop the three lengths of ribbon around the hoop and tie each in a knot. Suspend the hoop from the ceiling by slipping the ribbon loops over the hook. If your ribbon loops are spaced evenly around the hoop, the hoop will hang flat and parallel to the ceiling.

[2] Use string to approximate the distance from the hoop to the floor on each side of the bed, or use the measuring tape. Cut three pieces of netting that are each double this length.

[3] Thread each piece of netting through the ribbon loops. Arrange the material so there is good coverage all around the bed.

[4] Add color by attaching silk or plastic flowers or butterflies to the canopy. Push the stems or antennae carefully through the netting. Or tack in place with a needle and thread. Lounge in splendor.

# quillow

*It's a quilt! It's a pillow! It's both and so much more. Stitch an easy, cozy fleece throw that folds into its own pocket to make a handsome pillow. Use it to decorate your bed or make a comfy chair even more inviting.*

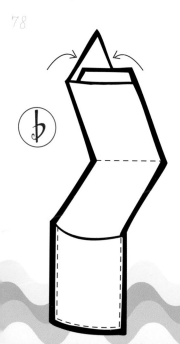

## You will need:

19-inch square of fleece, any color

Needle and thread or sewing machine

Scissors

Assorted decorating supplies: pieces of felt or fleece in contrasting colors, buttons, rickrack, ribbon, or puff paint (optional)

Fabric glue (optional)

48-by-60-inch piece of fleece in contrasting color

Straight pins

Embroidery thread and needle (optional)

1. The 19-inch square of fleece will form the face of the pillow when the blanket is folded inside. You may want to be fancy and decorate it. Some ideas to try:

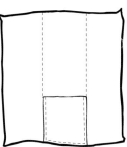

- Cut shapes such as hearts or stars from contrasting felt or fleece and stitch down or secure with fabric glue.
- Use puff paint to make swirls, zigzags, or letters.
- Sew on multicolored buttons.
- Stitch or glue on rickrack or ribbon.

2. Center the square of fleece, decorated side down, along the bottom edge of the larger piece of fleece (on the 48-inch side, not on the 60-inch side, see diagram a). Pin in place.

3. Using needle and thread or a sewing machine, stitch around the sides and bottom of the square, leaving 3/8-inch seam allowance all around. This will form your pocket.

4. To fold the quilt into its pocket, turn the quilt pocket-side down. Fold over sides along the side seams of pocket, then fold in thirds horizontally (see diagram b). Then turn pocket inside out, stuffing the quilt inside.

5. For a more finished look, embroider the edges with a contrasting color of embroidery thread. This step is easy, and the brightly colored thread makes for a big payoff with minimal effort. Check out some embroidery books from the library, or find an embroidery-savvy adult (they lurk among us) to give you a quick tutorial. Extra crafty!

# dazzling
## duvet

Does your bedding make you yawn? Wake up that tired old comforter with some snazzy do-it-yourself decorations. Check out our ideas or dream up some of your own.

### You will need:

Freshly laundered, old or store-bought duvet (solid colors look best)

Scissors

Assorted decorating supplies: felt, pom-pom trim, plastic insects and flowers, beads, fake pearls and gems, ribbon, silk, lace, rickrack, whatever

Needle and thread

Fabric glue (optional)

**Note**

If you can't find a store-bought duvet you like (or can afford), make your own by sewing together two flat sheets along the sides and top. Stitch some Velcro along the bottom edges for easy opening.

1 Get your duvet and your doodads and do it up! (If you're using the duvet currently adorning your bed, remove the comforter before proceeding.) Here are some decorating ideas:

## South-of-the-Border Bed

Cut cactus and sombrero shapes from felt. Stitch onto your duvet or secure with fabric glue. (When you are sewing decorations onto your duvet, be careful to not stitch through the top to the bottom.) Glue or stitch on a border of pom-pom trim.

## Bed Bugs

Stitch plastic dragonflies, butterflies, or colorful beetles around the edges of your duvet. Let one or two adventurous critters head for the center.

*continued on next page*

### Flower Bed

Stitch on silk flowers. Flat flowers such as daisies work well.

### Jewel-Box Bed

Sew beads onto your duvet. Try pearl polka dots or a random sprinkling of big sparkly gems. If your beads don't have holes, glue them to the duvet with fabric glue.

### Moon and Stars

Cut moon and star shapes from felt. Stitch onto your duvet or secure with fabric glue. This motif looks great on a dark-blue duvet. For an extra-special tableau, use glow-in-the-dark stars (craft stores sell these).

## Crazy Quilt

Anything goes. Sew or glue on strips of ribbon, lace, or rickrack trim. Stitch on special beads and patches of pretty silk. If you're really crafty, embroider flowers, dragonflies, or your name.

## Pocket Pastiche

Cut 8-inch squares of felt. Sew onto duvet to form pockets. Tuck your favorite stuffed animals or other treasures inside.

2   When your duvet is all decorated and the glue is all dry, stuff your old comforter back inside and crawl under the covers for a well-dressed catnap.

# ribbon-tie

## pillowcases

A girl shouldn't have to face unadorned pillows every night. Go out and find yourself a four-foot piece of beautiful ribbon and remedy the situation right now—you don't even need a sewing machine. Nice, wide, washable ribbon that looks sharp on both sides is the ticket.

### You will need:

Scissors

4 feet satin ribbon (1 inch or wider works best)

Clear nail polish

Ruler

Straight pins

Pillowcase

Needle and thread

1   Cut ribbon into four pieces, each one foot long. Cut one end of each piece into an inverted V-shape to prevent fraying. Seal the ends with clear nail polish and allow to dry.

Fold square end of ribbon under 1 inch and pin to open edge of the pillowcase, about 4 inches in from the edge. Pin the second ribbon in place on the opposite side of the opening. Sew each in place.

3 Repeat with remaining two pieces of ribbon on the other end of the pillowcase opening, 4 inches from the edge.

4 Put pillow inside and tie ribbons into lovely bows.

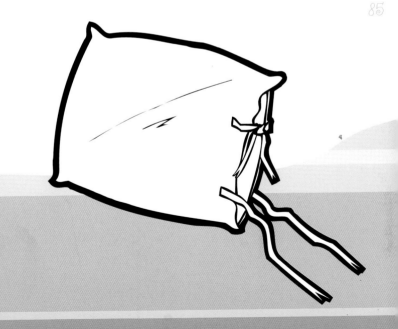

# hollywood safari
## pillow

**You will need:**

Straight pins

2 swatches of leopard-print fun fur, each 14-by-14-inches

Needle and thread

12-inch square pillow form

1   Pin fun-fur swatches together, fur sides facing in.

2   Sew around three edges, leaving a 1-inch seam allowance. Leave 1 inch unstitched on both sides and at the top.

[3] Turn right side out. Stuff pillow form inside, coaxing the pillow all the way into the corners of the cover.

[4] Fold unstitched edges under, pin closed, and stitch together. Toss on your bed and unwind. The paparazzi can wait.

# no-sew decorative

*pillows*

Is needle and thread a foreign language? Need to renovate your space pronto? Try this lightning-fast fix for dowdy old pillows. You'll be living in style before you can say "Hand me that scarf, sister." We've used a 12-inch square pillow, but any size pillow can be revamped; just look for a scarf with dimensions twice as big as the pillow's.

### You will need:

24-inch square scarf, ideally of shimmery silk in a gorgeous color or pattern, but any large scarf or big square of fabric will do

12-inch square pillow form or throw pillow, no matter how dull or ugly

1   Lay scarf on a flat surface. Place the pillow on the scarf (see diagram a).

2 Bring two opposite corners of scarf together and tie in a knot at center of pillow.

3 Bring the remaining scarf corners across pillow and knot together on top of the first knot (see diagram b). Presto, your pillow is reborn!

Note If you can't find a pretty scarf, take a trip to the fabric store. Explore the remnants (the cheaper "ends" of fabric bolts) or just buy a yard of colorful, inexpensive fabric.

89

a

b

sweet dreams

# sachet

Drifting off to sleep with the fragrance of rose petals or lavender practically guarantees a night of sweet dreams. This easy sachet will make your bedroom or closet smell like heaven. It also makes a pretty present.

## You will need:

12-inch length of velvet ribbon, 3 inches wide

Clear nail polish

Straight pins

Needle and thread

Potpourri, rose petals, or lavender flowers
(approximately 1½ cups)

1  Seal ends of ribbon with clear nail polish to prevent fraying.

2  Fold ribbon in half so it measures 6 by 3 inches. Make sure that velvety side faces in. Pin sides together.

3 Stitch long sides together, leaving ¹/₄-inch seam allowance. Stop stitching ¹/₂ inch from end on both sides.

4 Turn inside out. Fill with potpourri, rose petals, or lavender flowers.

5 Fold in ¹/₂ inch of fabric along top edge. Pin together and sew shut. Breathe deeply. Ahhhhh.

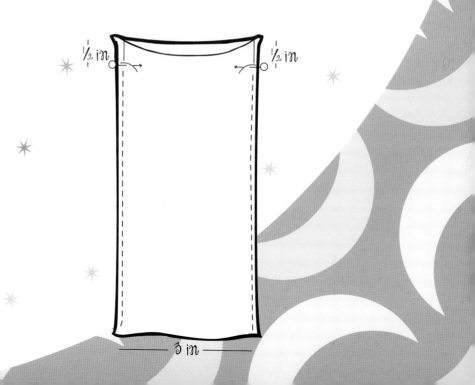

¹/₂ in          ¹/₂ in

3 in

part **5**

paper presents and
other cheap thrills

# custom

## coupons

We say, "I'll do anything for you," but do we really mean it? Even empty the cat box? Demonstrate your redeeming qualities with a gift book of coupons good for simple pleasures, extravagant gestures, and special snacks. Caution: Some folks have been known to actually use these coupons, so don't offer if you're not ready to follow through.

### You will need:

Ruler

Pencil

8½-by-11-inch sheet of card stock (stiff paper—1 sheet makes 8 coupons)

Scissors

Colored pens

Assorted decorating supplies: rubber stamps, stickers, glitter, paint, crayons, whatever

Old magazines (optional)

Hole punch

Ribbon

1 Using a ruler and light pencil line, divide card stock in half lengthwise. Cut stock along line.

2 Following the same procedure as in step 1, cut these two long pieces in half across their width, and then cut those pieces in half again to make eight equal rectangles.

3 On each rectangle, use colored pens to describe the goods or services that the coupon is offering. Here are some ideas:

- Breakfast in bed
- Car wash
- Homemade cookies
- Foot, hand, or neck massage with a fragrant oil or lotion
- Manicure or pedicure with fancy polish
- Read-aloud bedtime story
- Special Sunday brunch

*continued on next page*

4    Decorate each coupon with stamps, stickers, glitter, paint, drawings, magazine pictures, or whatever you like.

5    Hole-punch the coupons in the upper left-hand corner and fasten with a pretty ribbon.

Note    Give them the genie-in-a-bottle treatment: Roll three coupons, or "wishes," into slim tubes. Tie with pretty ribbon and slip into a decorative bottle.

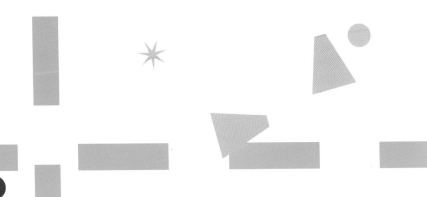

# gypsy-princess
# cootie catcher

Binder paper is fine for everyday cootie catchers, but special-occasion fortune telling calls for a zippier model. This grand take on the classic catcher uses gorgeous paper and embellishments and includes a ribbon, so you can tie it shut or carry it on your wrist. A dignified and intriguing accessory or party favor.

## You will need:

Ruler

Pencil

8-inch square of heavy art paper or stationery, any color

Pen

Scissors

Glue

Assorted decorating supplies: magazines, bits of lace, paper doilies, flat-back gems, stamps, metallic pen, stickers, glitter, whatever

2 lengths of ribbon, each 8 inches long

Needle and thread (optional)

*continued on next page*

[1] Using ruler and pencil, lightly draw two diagonal lines on the paper, one in each direction, intersecting in the center of the square.

[2] Fold the four corners in so they meet in the center where the two lines cross (see diagram a).

[3] Turn square over and repeat folding the corners in so they meet in the center (see diagram b).

[4] Turn over again to the side with four squares. Crease horizontally and vertically. Insert your fingers underneath the squares and pop into cootie catcher form.

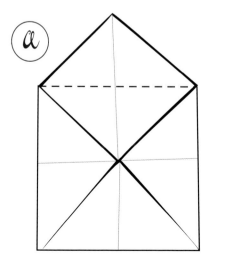

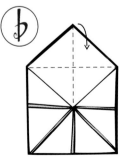

**5** Write in prompts and fortunes under the triangular flaps, in your best penmanship; or, for added mystery, type fortunes on an old typewriter, cut out, and paste in place. Here are some ideas for fortunes:

- Make a theme catcher, such as outdoor adventure (*You will hike to the top of a tall mountain*) or movies (*You will rent Benny and Joon numerous times for no particular reason*).
- Use drawings or magazine pictures instead of words to convey the fortune. A celebrity or love catcher might have Brad Pitt under one flap. A travel catcher could have a picture of the desert or New York City.
- Make a party catcher with festive fortunes such as, *Someone will tell you something very important. You will not understand it for many years;* or *Someone you meet tonight will become your dearest friend someday,* or *You will drink the last soda without knowing it.*

**6** Decorate. Cut lace or a doily into four pieces and glue on the outside for that gypsy-princess look. Glue a flat-back gem to each outer corner, stamp on pretty designs, draw on gold and silver curlicues, or make a flower border.

**7** Glue ribbons to opposite points and allow to set. You can also sew the ribbons in place.

# fancy stationery kit

E-mail and phone messages are great, but they can't compare to the feeling of seeing a letter in the mailbox, especially if it's decorated by hand. It's easy to design your own stationery, either for a special gift or as your trademark letterhead. Right on, write now.

## You will need:

6 sheets of pretty paper

Glue

Assorted decorating supplies: ribbon, rickrack, rubber stamps, colored pens, metallic pens, stencils, paints, crayons, pressed flowers, whatever

Ruler

6 envelopes

Plain stickers

Pencil

Scissors

8½-by-11-inch sheet of card stock (stiff enough to be used for postcards)

10-inch piece of ribbon

1. Decorate the six pieces of pretty paper. Don't forget to leave room for the letter part.
   Some cool ideas to try:
   - Glue on a ribbon border.
   - Rubber-stamp a pattern.
   - Draw a flowering vine.
   - Draw colored lines with a ruler for the text of the letter.
   - Create a monogram using calligraphy.
   - Make curlicues with a gold or silver pen.
   - Glue on pressed flowers.

2. Decorate the envelopes to match.

3. Decorate the stickers with hearts, flowers, drawings, slogans (*Hola chica! Ciao bella! Par Avion, Special Delivery, You're a star!*), or whatever.

4. Using ruler, pencil, and scissors, measure and cut card stock in quarters (each 4¼ by 5½ inches). On one side, draw lines for the "to" and "from" addresses and a box for the stamp. On the other side, decorate around the edges, leaving room in the middle for a short letter.

5. Assemble the paper, envelopes, stickers, and postcards as a packet and tie with the ribbon.

# peek-a-boo
# *greeting card*

*Thinking of that someone special? Make him or her a mini-masterpiece to say thank you, I miss you, or happy birthday.*

102

### You will need:

8½-by-11-inch sheet of card stock (stiff paper)

Ruler

Scissors

X-acto knife (caution: X-acto blades are sharp—ask an adult to help) and self-healing mat or newspaper (optional)

Glue

Photographs (silly ones are ideal) or magazines or newspapers to cut up for collage

Assorted decorating supplies: ribbon, rickrack, glitter, rubber stamps, stickers, fancy pens, paints, whatever

[1] Fold card stock in half to make a card.

[2] Using ruler and scissors, cut out a 2-by-3-inch window in front. The X-acto knife makes it much easier.

[3] Glue a photograph or magazine or newspaper picture to backside of front so you can see it through the window when the card is closed.

[4] Decorate the window frame however you like. Add the beginning of a message, such as *There's only one thing I have to say . . .* or *I was just thinking . . .*

[5] Inside, complete the message (*Happy Birthday! Thank You! You're the best! Friends are forever!*). Decorate the inside like a maniac.

# birthday

*scroll*

## You will need:

4½-by-20-inch sheet of paper (you can tape shorter lengths of paper together)

Fancy pen

Assorted decorating supplies: rubber stamps, stickers, glitter, whatever (optional)

Glue stick

2 toilet-paper tubes

Clothespins or binder clips

2 feet of pretty ribbon

1   Write your message in the center of the paper, leaving at least 4 inches at the top and bottom blank (to wrap around tubes). Use your best calligraphy and old-fashioned language: *By order of the palace, I hereby declare the birthday girl Queen for a Day. May all pay her tribute with cake and libations!* If you like, decorate with rubber stamps, stickers, or glitter. Add little drawings, curlicues, and flourishes.

By order of the palace, I hereby declare the birthday girl Queen for a Day. May all pay her tribute with cake and libations!

2 Glue a toilet-paper tube to each end of the paper, making sure that the tube is completely covered.

3 Secure with clothespins or binder clips to keep paper in place while glue dries. When glue is dry, remove clothespins.

4 Roll up and tie with ribbon.

# a gem of a journal

> You express yourself inside your journal, why not express your-self outside, too? Decorate it with souvenirs, drawings, and pictures of all the special things that make you you, such as your favorite animal (three-toed tree sloth), place (Swiss Alps), activity (glue-gun wielding), sport (rock climbing), or historical era (Ming Dynasty). It's all about you!

### You will need:

Store-bought journal (the plainer, the better)

Good craft glue, such as Aleene's Tacky Glue

Assorted decorating supplies (possibly including but certainly not limited to any of the following): fun fur, Astroturf (available at hardware stores), plastic crea-tures, silk flowers, felt cutouts (do-it-yourself kind), pictures and other mementos, découpage medium, flat-back beads and rhinestones, whatever

1. Grab your journal, your glue, and your doodads, and do it up. Some ideas to get you started:
   - Cut a piece of felt, fun fur, or Astroturf the same size as your journal, and glue to the cover. Add a row of rhinestones to the spine.
   - Assemble a collage of your favorite pictures, wrappers, movie stubs, notes, and other mementos and glue to the cover. Seal with several coats of découpage medium. Embellish with flat-back rhinestones.
   - Jewel your journal. Cover the cover with big flat-back gems.
   - Run amok with glue and a supply of plastic creatures, silk flowers, and felt cutouts.

2. When you're satisfied with the outside, get started on the inside. Pour your heart out. Document your environment, thoughts, experiences, and dreams. You might want to give yourself assignments: *If my life were a sitcom*, *When I am President,* or write a haiku about what happened during lunch. Or, if you don't feel like writing, document your day with artifacts: a wrapper from snack time, a hall pass, something you found on the way home. You don't need a special reason to contribute to your journal.

part 6

# the light fantastic

# aladdin's lamp

A little paint, a little Persia-inspired decoration, and suddenly that ugly old lamp is transformed into a luxury suite that any genie would be happy to inhabit.

## You will need:

Fabric paint in a bright color

Sponge brush

Old or store-bought ceramic lamp with plain fabric shade (you can buy a plain shade at a superstore if you already have the base)

Good craft glue, such as Aleene's Tacky Glue

Assorted grosgrain ribbons (bright colors that contrast with the paint are best)

Mini-mirrors

Sequins

**Note** If your lamp's base is ceramic, you may choose to paint it using a complementary shade of acrylic paint.

1. Using fabric paint and your sponge brush, give the lampshade a good coating of solid color. If you want a deeper tone, add another coat or two. Be sure to allow the paint to dry between coats.

2. When the paint is completely dry, glue the ribbons flat to your lampshade in any pattern you like. Glue them vertically or horizontally, spaced close or far apart.

3. Glue mini-mirrors and sequins on top of the ribbons in polka dot, zigzag, or diamond designs.

# lucky chinese
## lantern

*Celebrating the Chinese New Year includes the tradition of giving bright red envelopes containing money. The same envelopes make an enchanting paper lantern sure to bestow good fortune upon its maker. If you can't find a store that carries Chinese sundries, you can substitute any small, rectangular card that is attractive on both sides. For a Vegas touch, use playing cards.*

## You will need:

36 Chinese New Year money envelopes (or playing cards)

Clear tape

Tassel or charm (optional)

Needle and extra-strong red thread

1 Stand three envelopes up lengthwise (vertically) and tape together to make a triangle (see diagram a). Repeat five more times, so you end up with six tall triangles. Tape these six triangles together to form a hexagon. Try to tape on the inside, so it doesn't show.

2 Stand three envelopes up horizontally and tape together to make a shorter triangle (see diagram b). Repeat five more times, so you end up with six short triangles. Tape these triangles together to form a hexagon.

3 Place your short hexagon on top of the tall hexagon. Tape the two hexagons together (see diagram c). Attach the tassel or charm to the red thread and secure with tape to the bottom of the lantern.

4 With needle and red thread sew a loop on the top of the lantern, and hang. Happy New Year!

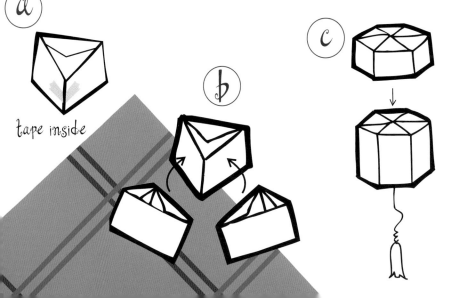

*a* tape inside

*b*

*c*

# floating-flowers
## *paper lantern*

The translucent white of an elegant paper lantern sets off your painted flowers in classic Japanese style. Make your lantern as simple or as elaborate as you wish. Even a few small, pink blossoms on a field of white makes for a serenely beautiful addition to your decor.

### You will need:

Nonflammable acrylic paint or watercolors and a small paintbrush

Paper lantern (any size will do; look for one at your local hardware store or world market)

Good craft glue, such as Aleene's Tacky Glue

Assorted decorating supplies: mini-mirrors, sequins, and flat-back beads

Needle and thread

Round beads and a charm

1. Paint a pretty flower pattern on your lantern. Daisies and vines are easy, or try petally pink cherry blossoms. Lotus blossoms are also fairly easy to paint. Look around the house, in the dictionary (under flower names), or at the library for simple flower motifs to copy. Add a butterfly or two.

2. Glue on mini-mirrors, sequins, and beads to accent your painting. Allow to dry.

3. String a charm or bright-colored button and 5 or 6 inches of beads on thread. Tie to bottom of lantern.

# va-va-voom
# votives

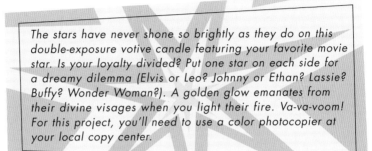

*The stars have never shone so brightly as they do on this double-exposure votive candle featuring your favorite movie star. Is your loyalty divided? Put one star on each side for a dreamy dilemma (Elvis or Leo? Johnny or Ethan? Lassie? Buffy? Wonder Woman?). A golden glow emanates from their divine visages when you light their fire. Va-va-voom! For this project, you'll need to use a color photocopier at your local copy center.*

### You will need:

2 magazine pictures of your favorite star or stars

Good craft glue, such as Aleene's Tacky Glue

Tall votive candle in glass holder (found in supermarkets and drugstores)

Assorted decorating supplies: flat-back gems, beads, tinsel, glitter, whatever

1   Whatever is on the back of the magazine pictures will shine through when the candle is lit, so unless the other side is blank, you will want to make color copies of the picture you want.

2 Glue one picture to either side of the glass.

3 Glue on flat-back gems, beads, tinsel, glitter, and whatever else you have on hand.

4 Allow to set. Once completely dry, turn down the lights, put on some mood music, and bask in the glow of your favorite heartthrob.

Note Never leave a burning candle unattended, even for a few minutes, and never go to sleep with it lit.

# disco ball

Dance the night away every day under your own disco ball. You'll feel the fever when you see the sparks fly off this glittery orb fashioned from ordinary materials. Change the regular lightbulb in an overhead light or lamp for a red or blue one, and suddenly your room is a disco sensation.

## You will need:

Styrofoam ball (8-inch diameter or bigger)

Acrylic craft paint (silver or any color)

Sponge brush

Good craft glue, such as Aleene's Tacky Glue

Assorted decorating supplies: mini-mirrors, sequins, glitter, flat-back gems, whatever

Screw hook

1 yard fishing line or strong thread

Pushpin for hanging (optional)

Blue or red lightbulb (optional—for ambiance)

1  Paint Styrofoam ball using sponge brush. Add more coats until it looks classy. Allow to dry.

2  Deck it out! Glue mini-mirrors, sequins, glitter, or flat-back gems all over it in swirl, zigzag, stripe, or curlicue patterns. You can't stop decorating until you drop!

3  Screw hook into the top of the ball. You may want to brush the hook with glue first to make it more secure. Let dry.

4  String fishing line or strong thread through hook and knot ends securely. Hang from ceiling by a pushpin or attach to an overhead light fixture.

5  Install blue or red lightbulbs in your lamp or light fixture and let the dancing begin!